To a True Champion

_____

From

_____

_____

_____

Date

I turn to the front pages of my newspaper
to read about men's failures.
I turn to the sport pages to read
about their triumphs.
—Oliver Wendall Holmes

A CHAMPIONSHIP LIFE

Thoughts for Men of Strength and Character

Written and Compiled by
Paul C. Brownlow

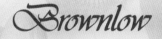

Brownlow

Blessed Men

In defending athletics I would not for
one moment be understood as excusing that
perversion of athletics that would make it the
end of life instead of merely a means of life.

–President Theodore Roosevelt

Blessed is the man who finds wisdom,
the man who gains understanding.

Proverbs 3:13

Sports do not build character. They reveal it.

–Heywood Broun

The golden age only comes to men
when they have forgotten gold.

—G. K. Chesterton

We do not want our children to become a generation
of spectators. Rather, we want each of them to become
participants in the vigorous life.

–President John F. Kennedy

A Championship Life

*T*rue champions are not necessarily the guys who
win the Final Four, the Super Bowl, or the U. S. Open.
A true champion is the man who played above his head,
playing better than his skill level should have allowed.
It is the guy who overcame more obstacles than most
just to compete—not necessarily to win. It is the man
who wanted to win, but was ready to lose rather than
sacrifice his integrity, moral courage, and honor.

This kind of person is seldom honored for his achievements,
but he is the true champion. And whether we possess athletic
ability or not, all of us can live a championship life. The
publicity and fame are less, but the rewards are greater—
not just in this life, but in the life to come.

–Paul C. Brownlow

One Stroke at a Time

*I*t is nothing new or original to say that golf is played one stroke at a time. But it took me many years to realize it.

—Bobby Jones

*C*onfidence is everything. From there, it's a small step to winning.

—Craig Stadler

I never pray on a golf course. Actually, the Lord answers my prayers everywhere except on the course.

—Lee Trevino

I could not shrink from a challenge. If the chance was there and if—no matter how difficult it appeared —it meant winning; I was going to take it. It was the sweetness of the risk that I remembered, and not its dangers. You must play boldly to win.

—Arnold Palmer

No Strangers, Only Friends

Having won the Open (1927) and the Amateur (1930) on the Old Course, Bobby Jones returned to St. Andrews for the last time in 1958. At that time, the city honored him with an award that only one other American, Benjamin Franklin, two hundred years earlier had ever received. Jones had captured their hearts, as well as their titles, like no other foreigner because of his flair for golf and the strength of his character.

That evening, the hall was full and Bobby (now crippled by a spinal disease) made his way to the podium to accept the award. Without notes and speaking from the heart, Jones concluded the emotional remarks by describing his thoughts on friendship:

Friends are a man's priceless treasures, and a life rich in friendship is full indeed. When I say, with due regard for the meaning of the word, that I am your friend, I have pledged to you the ultimate in loyalty and devotion. In some respects friendship may even transcend love, for in true friendship there is no place for jealousy. When I say that you are my friends, it is possible that I imposing upon you a greater burden than you are willing to assume. But when you have made me aware on many occasions that you have a kindly feeling toward me, and when you have honored me by every means at your command, then when I call you friend, I am at once affirming my high regard and affection for you and declaring my complete faith in you and trust in the sincerity of your expressions.

For those in attendance, it was a night of tears and memories never to be forgotten.

Small Fish and a Family

Govern a family as you would cook small fish—very gently.

—Chinese Proverb

The most important thing a father can do
for his children is to love their mother.

—Theodore Hesburgh

A child that is allowed to
be disrespectful to his
parents will not have
true respect for anyone.

—Anonymous

The absence of fathers is linked to most social
nightmares—from boys with guns
to girls with babies. No
welfare reform plan can
cut poverty as thoroughly
as a two-parent family.

—Joseph P. Shapiro and
Joanne M. Schrof

If you want your children
to turn out well, spend twice
as much time with them and
half as much money.

—Anonymous

The LORD *your God carried you, as a father carries his son, all the way you went until you reached this place.*

Deuteronomy 1:31

Insanity is hereditary; you can get it from your children.

—Sam Levenson

Most men I know have an instinct for fatherhood that was triggered the day their first child was born. They innately recognized the No. 1 requirement of fatherhood: be there.

—Fred Barnes

When an adult male truly understands the meaning of three words—time, commitment, and responsibility—then, in my opinion, he can call himself a father and a man.

—Dr. Wade Horn

The Words of a Champion

My parents got engaged at a football game. Now that's not very unusual you say, but my Dad never intended to get engaged that afternoon. He just sorta stumbled into it and was too embarrassed to back out.

They had been dating for a long time and my Mom thought he would never propose. As the game started, my Dad looked out over the field and surveyed the players. Then he leaned over and said, "Well, Ferne, I think Henry is going to be our best man."

She quickly grabbed her heart and replied, "Oh, this is so sudden. Let's set the wedding date right now!"

My Dad tells that for the truth, but I suspect the years have stretched part of the story. The one thing I do know is true, be careful of what you say. Words are more powerful than a bomb: they soothe, they hurt, they heal, and they destroy. They change things forever.

—Paul C. Brownlow

*T*he difference between the right word and the almost right word
is the difference between lightning and the lightning bug.

—Mark Twain

*W*ords—so innocent and powerless as they are, as standing
in a dictionary, how potent for good and evil they become
in the hands of one who knows how to combine them.

—Nathaniel Hawthorne

*E*ating words has never
given me indigestion.

—Winston Churchill

A man of knowledge uses words
with restraint and a man of
understanding is even-tempered.

Proverbs 17:27

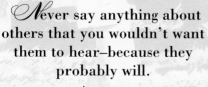

*N*ever say anything about
others that you wouldn't want
them to hear—because they
probably will.

—Anonymous

The Power of One

It's one-on-one out there, man.
There ain't no hiding,
I can't pass the ball.

—Pete Sampras

*E*very human being is intended to have a character
of his own; to be what no others are, and to do what
no other can do.

—William Ellery Channing

*E*very man carries his kingdom within, and no one knows
what is taking place in another's kingdom. "No one
understands me!" Of course they don't, each one of us
is a mystery. There is only one who understands you,
and that is God.

—Oswald Chambers

*C*arry your own lantern,
and you need not fear the dark.

—Jewish Proverb

I can do everything through him who gives me strength.

Philippians 4:13

*E*very single person has one thing that he can do
a little better than most people around him, and he has
a sacred obligation to himself to find out what that thing
is and to do it.

—Sydney J. Harris

Your Serve Ol' Sport

No wonder tennis was considered an elite sport for so long. The college tennis championship was won by a player from the Ivy League for thirty-seven of the first thirty-nine years (1883–1922). During that time Harvard won fifteen championships and Yale won nine.

Now college tennis has traded in its blue blazers for sun block. Teams from California routinely win the NCAA tennis championships with Stanford the dominant power for the last twenty years.

Tennis Shorts

You don't get there on natural ability alone.
A lot of people are born with natural ability,
but few of them become champions.
—Chuck McKinley

In a racquets game, you are like a boxer.
You attack and exploit another man's weakness.
And a five-set singles match would be like
going fifteen rounds.
—Stan Hart

You are never really playing an opponent.
You are playing yourself, your own highest standards,
and when you reach your limits, that is real joy.
—Arthur Ashe

Better Learn Baseball

*W*hoever wants to know the heart and mind of
America had better learn baseball.

—Jacques Barzum, French Philosopher

*I*f people don't want to come out to the ball park,
nobody's going to stop 'em.

—Yogi Berra

*T*he shortage of able-bodied men during
World War II caused the St. Louis Browns to put
one-armed Pete Gray in the outfield.
Pete played in seventy-seven games during 1945.

*T*hings could be worse. Our errors could
be counted and published in the newspaper
every day like those of baseball players.

*E*ddie Gaedel owns the record for the
shortest career in baseball. As a publicity
stunt on August 19, 1951, Eddie was sent in
as a pinch hitter for the St. Louis Browns.
At a height of only 3 feet 7 inches, Eddie's
presence caused the pitcher to nearly fall
down laughing. As a result, Eddie took four
pitches—all balls—and ran to first base.
He was then fired.

*You've gotta have
a lotta little boy in you
to play this game.*

—Roy Campanella

*Baseball gives every American boy
a chance to excel. Not just to be as
good as everyone else, but to be
better. This is the nature of the man,
and this is the name of the game.*

—Ted Williams

*W*hen it's played the way it is 'spozed to be played, basketball happens in the air; flying, floating, elevated above the floor, levitating the way oppressed peoples of the earth imagine themselves in their dreams.

—John Edgar Wideman

*T*he older I get, the better I used to be.

—Connie Hawkins

*G*uards win games, but forwards win championships.

—Anonymous

*O*nce a player becomes bigger than the team, you no longer have a team.

—Red Auerbach

*W*e were like the strings of a guitar. Each one was different, but we sounded pretty good together.

—Willie Worsley

*A*bility may get you to the top, but it takes character to keep you there.

—John Wooden

The Ref Doesn't Care

The trouble with basketball refs is that
they just don't care who wins.
—Tom Canterbury

They've had so many injuries,
they get to park their team bus
in the handicapped zone.
—George Ravelling

We have black players, white players,
a Mormon, and four Yugoslavians.
Our toughest decision isn't what offense
or defense to run, but what type
of warm-up music to play.
—Tim Capstraw

It's almost like the werewolf
syndrome. It's a full moon at home,
and guys play like werewolves.
Then we go on the road,
and it's a lunar eclipse.
—Ed Pinckney

We can't win at home.
We can't win on the road.
As general manager, I just can't
figure out where else to play.
—Pat Williams

Focused on the Goal

Too many golfers get concerned about what others do and forget to do what they have to do to play the game.

—Sam Snead

27.—J. E. LAIDLAY.

Obstacles are those frightful things you see when you take your eyes off the goal.

—Hannah More

It is important that you have road maps and blueprints in your life. It is a proven fact that people never exceed their goals. A person with a hazy goal never exceeds a hazy goal.

Without goals you have no stability; you are insecure in life. Goals give you desired power.

The great thing in this world is not so much where we stand as in what direction we are moving.

—O. W. Holmes

This one thing I do, forgetting those things which are behind, and reaching forth unto those things which are before, I press toward the goal.

Philippians 3:13–14

Most of us serve our ideals by fits and starts. The person who makes a success of living is the one who sees his goal steadily and aims for it unswervingly.

—Cecil De Mille

Our own happiness ought not to be our main objective in life.

—John Lubbock

A Great Catch

All you need to be a fisherman
is patience and a worm.
—Herb Shiner

A man who is master of patience
is master of everything else.
—Lord Halifax

A patient man has great understanding.
Proverbs 14:29

The key to everything is patience. You get the
chicken by hatching the egg—not by smashing it.
—Arnold Glasgow

A woman who has never seen her husband fishing
doesn't know what a patient man she has married.
—Ed Howe

The Trout, the Whole Trout, and Nothing But the Trout

A lie is a statement made with intent to deceive. No fisherman makes such statements. When another fisherman asserts that on a certain day he caught so many trout, we all know to divide the number and weight by three, half that, and knock off 90 percent of the quotient (or whatever it is). And when we retell the story to a third fisherman, we expect him to do likewise. Now such a man may not justly be accused of lying. He does no more than follow a well-recognized and convenient custom. This instinctive and generous discount which fishermen allow to one another's statements perfectly explains why those statements are so generously conceived.

It is cruel and wicked and quite unnecessary to assume that they are prompted by any sort of wish to deceive. If I tell another fisherman that I have caught—and I speak the very truth— sixteen trout weighing fifty ounces, he will think I have caught one fish weighing one ounce and risen two others of unknown size. And instead of his admiration, which is my due, I shall earn his contempt, which is unfair. In order to make him understand precisely what happened, I am compelled to speak in hundreds of fishes and in hundreds of pounds.

Fishermen are simply confirmed and painstaking truth tellers, who all happen to react a little feebly to a certain kind of stimulus. Now if it's liars you're looking for, don't search the banks of a stream. Go to the golf-links.

—William Caine

I'll Choose Character

I've seen the difference character makes in individual football players. Give me a choice between an outstanding athlete with poor character and a lesser athlete of good character, and I'll choose the latter every time. The athlete with good character will often perform to his fullest potential and be a successful football player, while the outstanding athlete with poor character will usually fail to play up to his potential and often won't even achieve average performance.

—Tom Landry

*C*haracter is not cut in marble; it is not something solid and unfaltering. It is something living and changing.

—George Eliot

*C*haracter is something each one of us must build for himself, out of the laws of God and nature, the examples of others, and—most of all—out of the trials and errors of daily life. Character is the total of thousands of small daily strivings to live up to the best that is in us.

—Lt. General A. G. Trudeau

*B*e on your guard; stand firm in the faith; be men of courage; be strong.

1 Corinthians 16:13

*C*haracter counts: more than any other factor it determines our reaction to adversity, temptation, sorrow, and approaching death. In every worthwhile aim it determines our success. It limits our influence over others, it decides our destiny; it— and not happiness—is the true end of life.

—Anonymous

Better Than Golf

Even golf is a trifling thing beside the privilege of taking a small son to the zoo and letting him see his first lion, his first tiger, and best of all, his first elephant.

—Heywood Broun

SEPT. '57

In golf there are no strangers, but only friends you've never met.

—Bill Campbell

A bad attitude is worse than a bad swing.

—Payne Stewart

Golf is 20 percent mechanics and technique. The other 80 percent is philosophy, humor, tragedy, romance, melodrama, companionship, camaraderie, cussedness, and conversation.

—Grantland Rice

A Better Game of Life

Our business in life is not to get ahead of other people, but to get ahead of ourselves. To break our own record, to outstrip our yesterdays by todays, to bear our trials more beautifully than we ever dreamed we could, to whip the tempter inside and out as we never whipped him before, to give as we never have given, to do our work with more force and a finer finish than ever— this is the true ideal—to get ahead of ourselves. To beat someone else in a game, or to be beaten, may mean much or little. To beat our own game means a great deal. Whether we win or not, we are playing better than we ever did before, and that's the point after all— to play a better game of life.

Take Me Out to the Ballgame

Well do I remember the afternoon (1845) when Alex Cartwright (a bank teller and volunteer fireman) came up to the ball field with a new scheme for playing ball. The sun shone beautifully; never do I remember noting its beams fall with a more sweet and mellow radiance than on that particular Spring day. For several years it had been our habit to casually assemble to play ball. We would take our bats and balls with us and play any sort of a game. We had no name in particular for it. Sometimes we batted the ball to one another or sometimes played one o' cat.

On this afternoon, Cartwright came to the field—the march of improvement had driven us further north and we located on a piece of property on the slope of Murray Hill (New York City) between the railroad cut and Third Avenue— with his plans drawn up on a paper. He had arranged for two nines, the ins and outs. He had laid out a diamond-shaped field, with canvas bags filled with sand or sawdust for bases at three of the points and an iron plate for the home base. He had arranged for a catcher, a pitcher, three basemen, a short fielder, and three outfielders. His plan met with much good-natured derision, but he was so persistent in having us try his new game that we finally consented more to humor him than with any thought of it becoming a reality.

—Duncan F. Curry

CHASE.N.Y.Amer.

Anything Can Happen

*The good Lord was good to me. He gave me a strong body,
a good right arm, and a weak mind.*

—Dizzy Dean

*As a boy I watched Saturday afternoon baseball with Dizzy Dean.
(No, I wasn't actually with Dizzy, he was on TV and I was at home.)*

*Dizzy had been a colorful player and naturally became a colorful TV
personality. He often told us that the runner had "slud" into third, or that
the batter was putting on his hamlet (helmet) before going into the batter's box.*

*But at the top of the ninth inning, no matter the score, Dizzy would say,
"Don't go away folks, anything can happen!" The score could be 0-15,
but Dizzy believed in persistence, determination, and that you never
give up until the game is over. I'd say that is a pretty good way to live.*

—*Paul C. Brownlow*

It Looks Like Coffee

Returning from a fishing trip, a man stopped at
a roadside diner and ordered a cup of coffee.
As he attempted to make conversation with
the waitress, he said, "It looks like rain, doesn't it?"

She promptly replied, "I can't help what it
looks like, we sell it for coffee."

Only Skilled Hands Eat Trout

It is to be observed that "angling" is the name
given to fishing by people who can't fish.

—Anonymous

Many men go fishing their entire lives without
knowing it is not the fish they are after.

—Henry David Thoreau

A smart wife has the pork chops ready for dinner
when her husband comes home from a fishing trip.

God never made a more calm, quiet,
innocent recreation than fishing.

—Izzak Walton (*The Complete Angler*, 1653)

If you would have a happy family life remember two things: in matters of principle, stand like a rock; in matters of taste, swim with the current.
—Anonymous

There's nothing wrong with teenagers that reasoning with them won't aggravate.
—Anonymous

Forget quality time. You can't plan magic moments or bonding or epiphanies in dealing with kids. What matters is quantity time.
—Fred Barnes

Fathers, do not embitter your children, or they will become discouraged.
Colossians 3:21

If a man is truly blessed, he returns home from fishing to be greeted by the best catch of his life.
—Anonymous

How to Be a Champion

*I*f you're going to be a champion, you must be willing
to pay a greater price than your opponent.
—Bud Wilkinson

I learned that if you want to make it bad enough,
no matter how bad it is, you can make it.
—Gale Sayers

*I*t's not whether you get knocked down,
it's whether you get up.
—Vince Lombardi

*N*ever go to bed a loser.
—George Halas

You never really lose until you stop trying.

—Mike Ditka

If you don't invest much, defeat doesn't hurt
and winning is not exciting.

—Dick Vermeil

You play the way you practice.

—Pop Warner

For every pass I ever caught in a game,
I caught a thousand in practice.

—Don Hutson

The first time you quit, it's hard.
The second time, it gets easier.
The third time, you don't even have to think.

—Paul "Bear" Bryant

Been on Hee Haw Lately?

E. L. BARTLEET

Captain Leion

*Y*ears ago, an egotistical and popular rising young star of the professional tennis circuit was traveling through a small airport in Kentucky. As he was checking in, he asked the ticketing agent what security the airline would be providing for him and his entourage. The agent just looked at him and replied, "Honey, this is Northern Kentucky, unless you've been on Hee Haw lately, you ain't got nothing to worry about."

When we're getting a little too full of ourselves, maybe we need to remember we ain't been on Hee Haw lately either.

—Melissa Reagan

*B*ut with humility comes wisdom.

Proverbs 11:2

*O*ne nice thing about egotists:
They don't talk about other people.

—Lucille S. Harper

*A*fter crosses and losses,
men grow humbler and wiser.

—Benjamin Franklin

*W*hoever humbles himself will be exalted.

Matthew 23:12

A man can counterfeit love, he can counterfeit faith, he can counterfeit hope and all the other graces, but it is very difficult to counterfeit humility.

—Dwight L. Moody

*H*umility is to make a right estimate of one's self.

—Charles H. Spurgeon

*P*ride kills thanksgiving, but a humble mind is the soil out of which thanks naturally grows. A proud man is seldom a grateful man, for he never thinks he gets as much as he deserves.

—Henry Ward Beecher

*T*he first test of a truly great man is his humility. I do not mean by humility, doubt of his own power. But really great men have a curious feeling that the greatness is not in them, but through them. And they see something divine in every other man and are endlessly, foolishly, incredibly merciful.

—John Ruskin

*I*t's a good idea to begin at the bottom in everything except in learning to swim.

—Anonymous

One Cliché at a Time

*E*very athlete worth his weight in sports drinks and Nike endorsements has to learn to say the all-time sports cliché. They not only have to learn to say it, but to act like they even believe it. Now, once more with feeling, "We're not gonna overlook anybody. We're gonna play 'em one game at a time."

While sports championships are indeed won by this simple philosophy, it also applies to life. In fact, one day at a time works better in life than in sports. After all, sports are fun, but life is for keeps. Resist the urge to dwell on future problems or past regrets. Remind yourself every day when you get up, today is a gift from God. Use it wisely. Cherish your family. Laugh at least once an hour. Call someone you love. Find something to be grateful for. Do something nice for somebody who isn't expecting it. Talk to God about what is going on in your world.

—Paul C. Brownlow

What we know as the NBA began in 1937 with thirteen teams coming together as the National Basketball League (NBL). Three corporations in the Akron, Ohio, area formed it: General Electric, Firestone, and Goodyear. In 1949 the teams merged with the young Basketball Association of America (BAA) to create the NBA. The oldest surviving teams are:

Teams	First Season	League Titles	Home Cities
Atlanta Hawks	1946-47	1 NBA (1958)	Tri-Cities (1946-51)
			Milwaukee (1951-55)
			St. Louis (1955-68)
			Atlanta (1968-)
Boston Celtics	1946-47	16 NBA	Boston (1946-)
		(1957, 59-66, 68-69,	
		74, 76, 81, 84, 86)	
Detroit Pistons	1941-42	2 NBL (1944-45)	Fort Wayne (1941-57)
		2 NBA (1989-90)	Detroit (1957-)
Golden St. Warriors	1946-47	1 BAA (1947)	
		2 NBA (1956, 75)	Philadelphia (1946-62)
			San Francisco (1962-71)
			Oakland (1971-)
Los Angeles Lakers	1947-48	1 NBL (1948)	Minneapolis (1947-60)
		1 BAA (1949)	Los Angeles (1960-)
		12 NBA (1950, 52-54,	
		72, 80, 82, 85, 87-88,	
		00-01)	
New York Knicks	1946-47	2 NBA (1970, 73)	New York (1946-)
Philadelphia 76ers	1949-50	3 NBA (1955, 67,83)	Syracuse (1949-63)
			Philadelphia (1963-)
Sacramento Kings	1945-46	1 NBL (1946)	Rochester (1945-58)
		1 NBA (1951)	Cincinnati (1958-72)
			KC-Omaha (1972-75)
			Kansas City (1975-85)
			Sacramento (1985-)

A Father's Touch

Bob Feller, the Cleveland ace, recalls how his Dad found ways to save time on the farm so he could help his son learn the game of baseball:

He pitched batting practice to me, even built me a batting cage out of leftover lumber and chicken wire. Later he caught me when I pitched. This was practically every night, after our farm chores were done. During cold or rainy weather, we'd play in the barn. He'd have me pitching under game conditions with a dummy batter.

He bought me proper equipment too; uniform, spikes, a good glove always and official league balls, not the nickel rocket variety that a lot of my friends had to use.

And we talked and talked about baseball, studied books on the fine points of the game, sitting around our big warm kitchen.

Probably the greatest thing he did for me was when I was twelve, we built a complete ball field on our farm. We called it Oakview 'cause it was up on a hill overlooking the Raccoon River and a beautiful view of a grove of oak trees. We had a complete diamond with an outfield fence and score-board and even a grandstand behind first base.

The Power of Adversity

Many men owe the grandeur of their lives
to their tremendous difficulties.

—Charles H. Spurgeon

We know that suffering
produces perseverance and
perseverance produces
character.
Romans 5:3

JOHN M. WARD.
ALLEN & GINTER'S
RICHMOND. Cigarettes VIRGINIA.

CHAS. W. BENNETT.
ALLEN & GINTER'S
RICHMOND. Cigarettes VIRGINIA.

In college at UCLA, Jackie Robinson
lettered in four sports: baseball,
football, basketball, and track.
Baseball was his weakest sport,
but the one by which he became
famous. During his first season with
the Dodgers, he was lonely, he was a pioneer,
and he was scrutinized for every flaw and every weakness.
But he endured. As Roger Kahn said, "Jackie bore the burden
of a pioneer and the weight made him more strong."

Mulligans

*T*he uglier a man's legs are, the better he plays golf
—it's almost a law.
—H. G. Wells

*T*here are two things that made golf appealing to the average man:
Arnold Palmer and the invention of the mulligan.
—Bob Hope

I don't say my golf game is bad, but if I grew tomatoes,
they'd come up sliced.
—Miller Barber

$\mathcal{T}$he good thing is, I don't have to play Tiger Woods
until I'm ninety.
—Chi Chi Rodriquez

$\mathcal{G}$olf combines two favorite American pastimes:
taking long walks and hitting things with a stick.
—P. J. O'Rourke

$\mathcal{I}$'m about five inches from being an outstanding golfer.
That's the distance between my left ear and my right.
—Ben Crenshaw

Are You Ready for
Some Fathering?

After getting my first chance to change
your diaper, I brought you back downstairs.
I turned on the television, and as luck would
have it, the San Francisco 49ers were playing.
I turned out all the lights, lay down on the
couch, and put you on my chest. I was so
afraid that my big hands were going to drop
you, but I held on. It wasn't five minutes
later that you fell asleep, holding my
finger. It was at that moment I realized
that I was a dad.

—John Barnet

A boy is the only thing God will use to make a man.

—Anonymous

*W*hen alone, guard your thoughts; in the family guard your temper; in company guard your words.

—Anonymous

*L*isten my son to your father's instruction and do not forsake your mother's teaching.

Proverbs 1:8

*O*ne hundred years from now, it will not matter what kind of car I drove, what kind of house I lived in, how much money I had, nor what my clothes looked like. But the world may be a little better, the universe a little brighter, because I was important to a child.

—Anonymous

Finishing Strong

*Y*ears ago, we took a vacation to Aspen in October.
We took the boys out of school, got their homework
assignments, and headed out. We found an old cabin
by a stream and made it home for a week.

During the mornings we had school and in the
afternoons we played football and scrambled
about the nearby river.

But at night, we all four got under Red Cover
(the big red blanket with cowboys on it) and watched
the World Series. I've forgotten the year, but it was
one of those years that Reggie Jackson earned his title
as Mr. October. It was amazing! And no matter what
you think of Reggie, his World Series appearances
will not soon be equaled or forgotten.

As I get older, I think about rising to the occasion
and finishing strong. I want my last years as a husband,
a father, a Sunday school teacher, a friend, a mentor,
and a businessman to be my best. I've got
a little Reggie left in me yet.

—Paul C. Brownlow

*B*ear in mind, if you are going to amount to anything, that your success does not depend upon the brilliancy and the impetuosity with which you take hold, but upon the everlasting and sanctified bull-doggedness with which you hang on after you have taken hold.

—A. B. Meldrum

*B*lessed is the man who perseveres, because when he has stood the test, he will receive the crown of life that God has promised to those who love him.

James 1:12

*F*ar better is it to dare mighty things, to win glorious triumphs even though checkered by failures, than to rank with those poor spirits who neither enjoy much nor suffer much because they live in the gray twilight that knows not victory or defeat.

—Theodore Roosevelt

*W*hat we obtain too easy, we value too lightly; it is the cost that gives value.

—Anonymous

*N*ever give in! Never give in! Never! Never! Never! Never! In anything great or small, large or petty—never give in except to convictions of honor and good sense.

—Sir Winston Churchill